HOW? WHO? WHAT? WHEN? WHERE? WHY?

Questions
kids
ask

ABOUT
SNAKES, FROGS &
THEIR RELATIVES

Questions Kids Ask . . . about SNAKES, FROGS & THEIR RELATIVES

continued

What are amphibians?

What do frogs, toads and salamanders have in common? They are all amphibians. Amphibians are animals that live a double life. In fact, the name "amphibian" comes from the Greek words *amphi,* meaning both, and *bios,* meaning life. Most amphibians begin their life in the water breathing through gills like a fish. As they mature, their body changes shape and they develop lungs. They can now live in the water and on land.

Amphibians do not drink water —they absorb it through their skin. For this reason they must keep themselves moist at all times. These clammy creatures are cold-blooded and in the north they hibernate in the winter.

What are reptiles?

You may be surprised to discover that snakes, lizards, turtles and crocodiles are all reptiles. The word "reptile" means *creeping.* Although not all these creatures creep, and they certainly don't look alike, they have many things in common. They all have backbones and dry, scaly skin, they breathe air through lungs and they are cold-blooded. Most reptiles have four legs with five clawed toes at the end of each. While a few species inhabit cool areas, many of them live in tropical or temperate regions.

Why do snakes stick out their tongues?

Have you ever wondered why a snake keeps flicking its tongue in and out of its mouth? It is not trying to sting, nor is it giving you a "raspberry." Believe it or not, snakes not only taste but smell with their tongues!

A snake can stick out its tongue without opening its mouth, thanks to a notch in the upper lip. As the snake crawls along, it constantly sticks its tongue out of this hole and feels its way along the ground. At the same time its forked tip picks up tiny scent particles on the ground and in the air, and carries them to a place on the roof of the snake's mouth where there is a special organ for smell and taste. This very effective method of smelling enables the snake to follow the scent trail left by its prey, to sample food or find a mate. When its tongue is not being used, the snake pulls it into a sheath in its mouth for safe keeping.

How many snakes are poisonous?

Poisonous to whom? Many snakes carry enough poison to kill small animals but not enough to bother a human being. Other snakes can kill a person with a single drop of venom. There are 2500 to 3000 different species of snakes, but only 270 may be harmful or fatal to people. In North America some of these are coral snakes, cottonmouths, copperheads and rattlesnakes— the most dangerous being the eastern diamondback rattlesnake.

Do snakes spit?

Some do and some don't. The spitting cobras of southern Africa have the ability to spit a stream of venom as far as 2 metres (6 feet). The poison is aimed at the eyes of any animal close enough to make the snake feel threatened. The victim is temporarily blinded by the poison, and if it isn't washed out right away, this blindness can be permanent.

Spitting cobras spit as a means of self-defense. They have strong muscles encasing the glands that make and store their poison. When the muscles tense, a fine stream of venom is forced out under pressure from the holes in the fangs. Spitting cobras hunt small animals, which they bite in the usual way. Fortunately, they are the only snakes that spit, and you have to go to southern Africa to find them.

You make me so mad I could spit.

DID YOU KNOW . . . snakes continue to grow all their lives.

This is the only way to fly!

Can frogs breathe under water?

If you have ever tried to catch a frog, you know how long it can hide under water. It's hard to believe that any creature could hold its breath so long. Why doesn't the frog have to come to the surface for air?

Believe it or not the frog is still breathing down there at the bottom of the pond—though not through its nose and mouth as it does above water. Frogs have soft, moist skin that contains a vast network of blood vessels. Incredibly, oxygen from the water passes through the skin directly into the frog's blood!

So if you are ever waiting for a frog to come up for air . . . don't hold your breath!

Can frogs fly?

Apart from insects, only birds and bats are true flyers, but many animals can do the next best thing —glide through the air. The most unusual of the skydivers are the incredible flying frogs of Asia. These lightweight aerialists can make fantastic flying leaps of up to 15 metres (50 feet)! By making their bodies concave and spreading their oversized fingers and toes, they glide effortlessly from tree to tree.

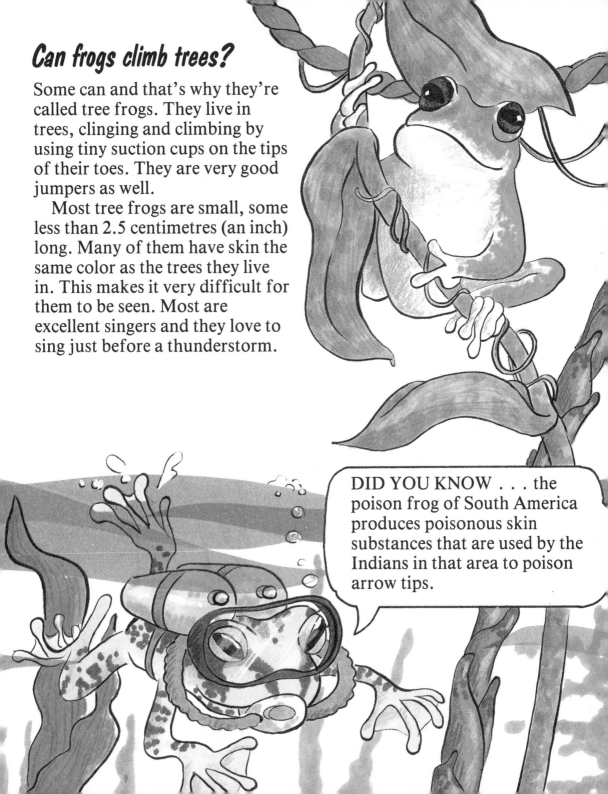

Can frogs climb trees?

Some can and that's why they're called tree frogs. They live in trees, clinging and climbing by using tiny suction cups on the tips of their toes. They are very good jumpers as well.

Most tree frogs are small, some less than 2.5 centimetres (an inch) long. Many of them have skin the same color as the trees they live in. This makes it very difficult for them to be seen. Most are excellent singers and they love to sing just before a thunderstorm.

DID YOU KNOW . . . the poison frog of South America produces poisonous skin substances that are used by the Indians in that area to poison arrow tips.

How long can a turtle hold its breath?

Would you believe several weeks or even a few months? Here's how.

A turtle doesn't have automatic body temperature control like birds and mammals. Its temperature changes according to its surroundings. When it gets too cold for a turtle's liking, it burrows deep into the mud at the bottom of a pond or into the dirt of the forest.

How can it breathe when it's buried? The turtle stops breathing air directly. Instead it takes in air through its skin, throat and through an opening under its tail. And when spring comes and the ground warms up, the turtle digs itself out and starts breathing normally again.

Can you tell the age of a turtle by its shell?

Sometimes you can—but you'd be wise not to make any bets.

In areas where a turtle's growth is seasonal, it may show rings on its shell like the growth rings of trees. It is therefore possible to tell the age of such turtles by counting the rings—at least while they are young. As a turtle grows older, however, the rings fade and may even wear off completely. So don't expect to be able to count the rings on a 123-year-old turtle.

Can a turtle leave its shell?

No, and it doesn't want to because a turtle's shell is part of its body. The inner layer of the shell is part of the backbone and the ribs. The outside is covered in large scales made up of a hard material like your fingernails. The shell grows along with the turtle, so it never feels cramped.

And the shell provides armored protection. Some turtles can pull their legs, tail and head completely inside their shell at the first sign of danger. This may be one reason why turtles have been around since the time of the dinosaurs.

DID YOU KNOW . . . a North American box turtle can support 200 times its weight on its shell—that's the same as if a person could bear the weight of two large elephants!

That's a great weight off my back.

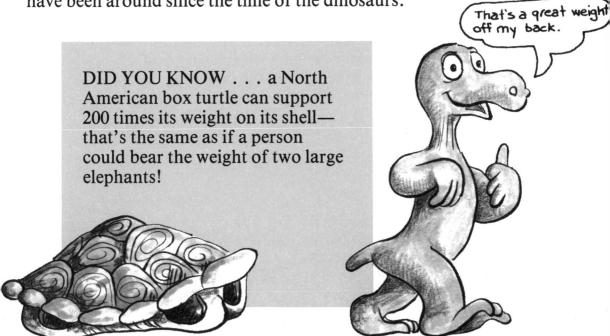

What reptile is referred to as a living fossil?

The tuatara lives on small islands off the coast of New Zealand. It is the last remaining member of the order *Rhynchocephalia* which was widespread 200 million years ago. The tuatara has a crest of spines that runs from its head to the tip of its tail and a loose-fitting scaly skin of brownish green. It lives in grass-lined chambers in underground burrows that it sometimes shares with birds. It sleeps all day and comes out at night to eat insects and snails.

What is a blindworm?

Did you think that a blindworm must be a worm that can't see? It may surprise you to discover that a blindworm isn't blind—it's not even a worm. A blindworm is the common name for a type of lizard that lives in Europe, western Asia and Algeria. It's usually about 30 centimetres (a foot) long and has no legs. This makes it look like a long worm. Smooth, round scales cover its body and it crawls around like a snake, looking for food with its tiny eyes. Blindworms live in grassy banks and ditches. They are one of the few animals that eat mostly slugs.

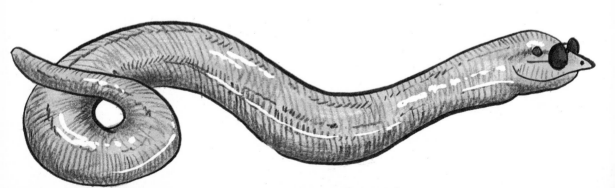

What is a Gila monster?

The Gila (pronounced heeluh) monster is a poisonous lizard. It can't stab or strike the way snakes can. Instead the poison flows between the lip and lower jaw before it reaches its grooved teeth. So the Gila monster has to hold on tightly to its prey with both jaws and give time for the poison to flow into the wounds. It has a bulldog grip—you often have to use pliers to get the jaws apart! Although its bite is rarely fatal to humans, it is extremely painful. But don't worry. Gila monsters don't eat people. They eat mainly eggs, birds, small mammals and other lizards. They can go without food for months by living on the fat stored in their thick tail.

What is the world's largest snake?

If you are afraid of snakes you would not want to meet the anacondas of South America. These monsters can grow up to 9 metres (30 feet) long! The largest one ever captured measured 11.5 metres (38 feet) long and weighed 455 kilograms (1000 pounds). These enormous water snakes are not poisonous. They kill their prey by wrapping themselves around it and squeezing. Eventually their victims suffocate and are swallowed whole.

Another exceptionally large snake is the reticulated python, which makes its home in the jungles of Asia, Indonesia and the Philippine Islands. These snakes commonly reach a length of 6 metres (20 feet) but are much thinner than the anaconda. The largest python measured so far was an impressive 10 metres (32 feet) long!

Do all snakes have fangs?

Snakes have a large number of teeth—80 or more. These thin, needle-like teeth are used to hold prey and to pull it into the snake's throat.

Some snakes have special teeth called fangs. These are hollow, like hypodermic needles, and venom flows through them. The cobra and viper families are the only snakes that have true fangs. Cobras have short fangs so they must jab awkwardly at their victims and can't strike as quickly as vipers. Vipers, which include rattlesnakes and moccasins, have long fangs. The fangs fold back in the snake's mouth when not in use.

It doesn't matter whether you meet a snake with short or long fangs—you won't want to stick around.

DID YOU KNOW . . . there are snake fossils from the time of the dinosaurs that are more than 18 metres (60 feet) long.

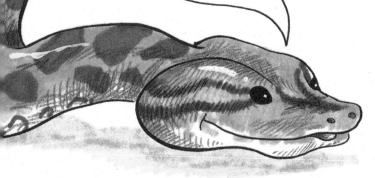

YIKES!

What is the world's shortest snake?

The shortest snake in the world is the tiny, harmless thread snake, which makes its home on the islands of Martinique, Barbados and St. Lucia in the West Indies. To date, the *largest* one ever officially documented measured just over 12 centimetres (4-1/2 inches). The shortest venomous snake, the spotted dwarf adder found in southwestern Africa, is about twice as long, with adults that average 23 centimetres (9 inches).

What is a salamander?

It is an amphibian with a short body, four legs and a tail. Salamanders range in size from 10 centimetres (4 inches) to 180 centimetres (70 inches). They have large eyes and a large mouth and they find slugs, snails, beetles and worms delicious. Even though they never drink water, salamanders have moist, slippery skin. They can absorb water and oxygen through their skin.

Salamanders are shy creatures who spend a lot of their lives hiding. They are active mainly when it is dark. So although some salamanders may be living in a woodpile near your house or in a forest where you often walk, you may never see them.

What is the difference between a newt and a salamander?

A newt is a kind of salamander. Newts have thick, rough, textured skin unlike most other salamanders. They have long, slender bodies and a tail that is flattened. They spend the early part of their lives in the water.

Newts are the most popular kind of salamander for pets. The best-known newt hatches in water and then spends two or three years on land as the red eft. Then it returns permanently to water, changing color to green.

DID YOU KNOW . . . not only can salamanders grow new tails if the old one is removed, they can even grow a new arm or leg if they lose one!

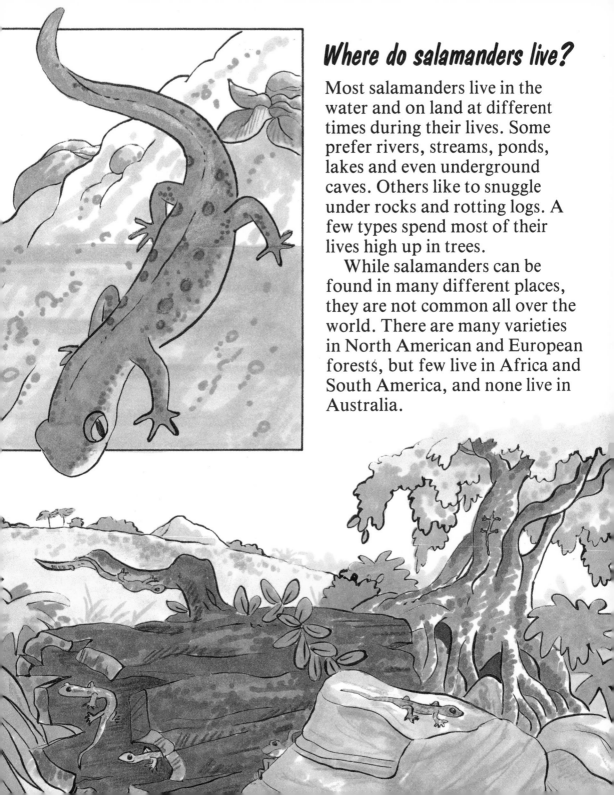

Where do salamanders live?

Most salamanders live in the water and on land at different times during their lives. Some prefer rivers, streams, ponds, lakes and even underground caves. Others like to snuggle under rocks and rotting logs. A few types spend most of their lives high up in trees.

While salamanders can be found in many different places, they are not common all over the world. There are many varieties in North American and European forests, but few live in Africa and South America, and none live in Australia.

What is the difference between an alligator and a crocodile?

Alligators and crocodiles both belong to an ancient order of reptiles known as the crocodilians. Although many people use the word alligator for all kinds of crocodilians, there are only two species of true alligator. One is the American alligator, which lives in the swamps of the southern United States, and the other is the rare and much smaller Chinese alligator. There are, however, over a dozen species of crocodile.

The main difference between crocodiles and alligators is that crocodiles are more active and aggressive than the sluggish alligator. Some crocodile species frequently kill and eat large animals, and occasionally even

people. Should you be close enough to one of these animals, and brave—or foolish—enough to try to find out which kind it is, look at the mouth. (Probably you wouldn't be able to look at anything else!) In crocodiles the fourth tooth on each side of the lower jaw is enlarged, and it sticks out when the jaws are closed. Alligators have broader, rounder snouts than crocodiles, and different jaws. All the alligator's teeth fit inside its mouth when the mouth is closed. Mind you, that doesn't help you much if the mouth is open . . .

Watch out Mom!

DID YOU KNOW . . . 120 million years ago crocodiles were 12 metres (40 feet) long and they ate dinosaurs!

Can lizards grow new tails?

Lizards have many different ways to defend themselves, but one of the strangest ways is by shedding their tail. When captured, a lizard can confuse its enemy by leaving its tail behind. The tail wiggles as if alive, while the lizard escapes. A new tail grows quickly, though often not the same color or size as the original.

Occasionally a lizard will break off its tail for another reason—it's hungry. When food is very scarce, some types of lizard will eat their own tail to avoid starvation.

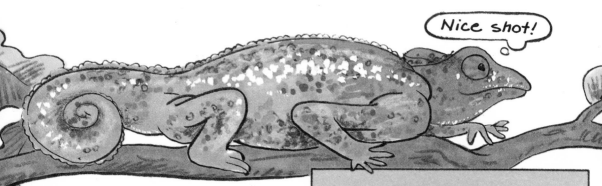

Nice shot!

Why does a chameleon change color?

Chameleon is the name of a group of lizards that live mainly in Madagascar and Africa. Chameleons are known for their ability to change color.

It was once believed that they changed color to match their surroundings to hide themselves from enemies. This is not true. A chameleon changes color in response to its moods, the temperature or light conditions.

DID YOU KNOW . . . glass snakes, which are really burrowing lizards with no legs, can break their tails into several pieces—just like glass!

The main color of most chameleons is brown or green. They can turn off-white, yellow or light green. When chameleons are cold, they turn light. When they are hot, they become dark. And when a chameleon is excited or frightened, it becomes covered in dark *and* light patches.

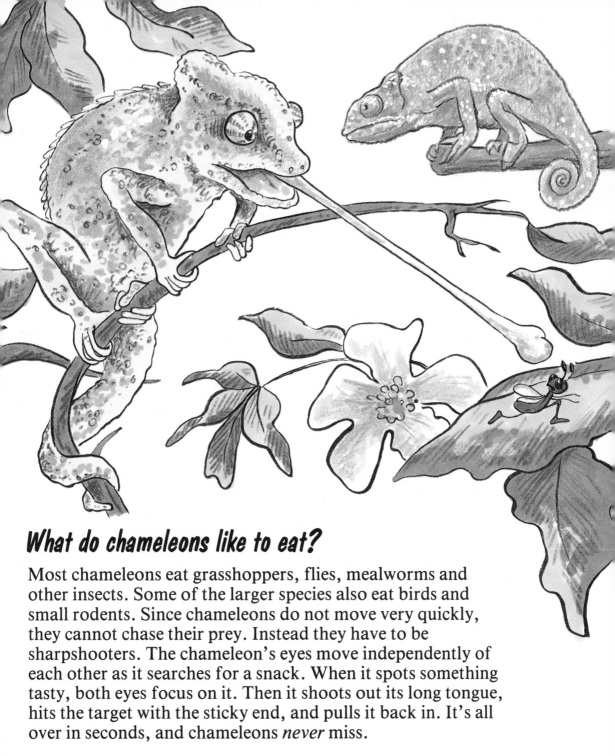

What do chameleons like to eat?

Most chameleons eat grasshoppers, flies, mealworms and other insects. Some of the larger species also eat birds and small rodents. Since chameleons do not move very quickly, they cannot chase their prey. Instead they have to be sharpshooters. The chameleon's eyes move independently of each other as it searches for a snack. When it spots something tasty, both eyes focus on it. Then it shoots out its long tongue, hits the target with the sticky end, and pulls it back in. It's all over in seconds, and chameleons *never* miss.

Should I tell her I'm not a prince?

Do toads give you warts?

In a popular fairytale, a beautiful princess kisses a toad and—presto —it turns into a handsome prince! Should you decide to kiss a toad you are about as likely to have the same thing happen to you as you are to get warts. Contrary to popular belief, it is impossible to get warts by touching a toad. However, the toad does emit a poison through the lumps on its skin, in order to discourage other animals from eating it. While this liquid is not normally harmful to us it can be quite irritating to our eyes. For this reason you should be careful to wash your hands after touching a toad.

How do frogs and toads sing?

Each spring the swamps and ponds come alive with a chorus of singing frogs and toads. Have you ever wondered how these little minstrels make their music? Believe it or not, they actually sing with their mouths and nostrils closed!

A frog or a toad gets ready to give its concert by taking a deep breath. Then it simply pumps the air back and forth through its voice box and into a sac in its throat or on the side of its head. In some species, this vocal sac inflates enormously and can get almost as big as the animal itself!

The calls of the various frogs and toads are as distinctive as those of birds. Some whistle or chirp, while others trill or peep.

One species of frog actually barks like a dog! But the most familiar voices of all are the steady tremolo of the common toad and the loud "jug-o-rum" of the deep-voiced bullfrog.

DID YOU KNOW . . . it is usually only the male frogs and toads we hear singing. Most females have very weak voices or none at all.

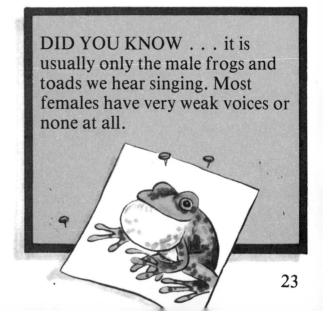

23

Are there sea snakes?

There are sea snakes in the tropical waters of the Indian Ocean and the western Pacific Ocean, but they are much smaller than the monstrous sea serpents that sailors used to fear.

Most sea snakes live in the shallow waters along the coasts of Australia and Asia. They are usually less than a metre (3 feet) long, although some types can reach 2.5 metres (8 feet). They have oar-like tails, flattened bodies, and nostrils on top of their snouts. Although sea snakes possess a very strong toxic poison that they use to kill eels and fish, they rarely bite people.

DID YOU KNOW . . . sea snakes are considered a delicacy in Japan where they are smoked and eaten with soy sauce.

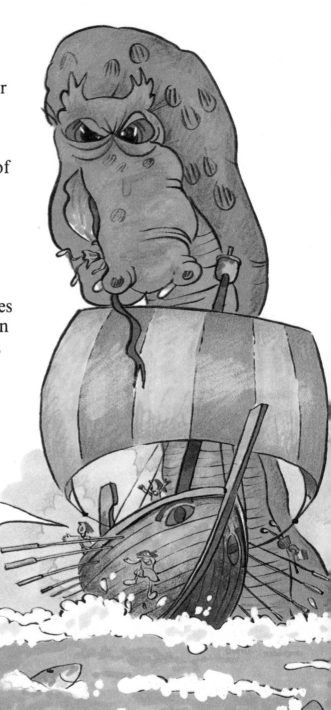

Why do rattlesnakes have rattles?

Rattlesnakes have rattles so that they can warn you to keep away. No snake wants to be stepped on, and nobody wants to step on a snake, so the rattle is good for everyone.

There are 30 different types of rattlesnakes and most of them live in North America. They range from the small massasauga rattlesnake of Ontario, which eats frogs and is rarely more than 30 centimetres (one foot) long, to the large and very dangerous eastern diamondback rattlesnake that lives in the southern United States and can grow to be 3 metres (9 feet) long or more.

DID YOU KNOW . . . rattlesnakes can't hear their own rattles because they have no external ears to pick up sounds that travel through the air.

Rattlesnakes come out of the egg with a single button rattle or ring at the end of the tail. Each time they shed their skin another segment is added. The buzzing or rattling sound comes from these dry rings rubbing together.

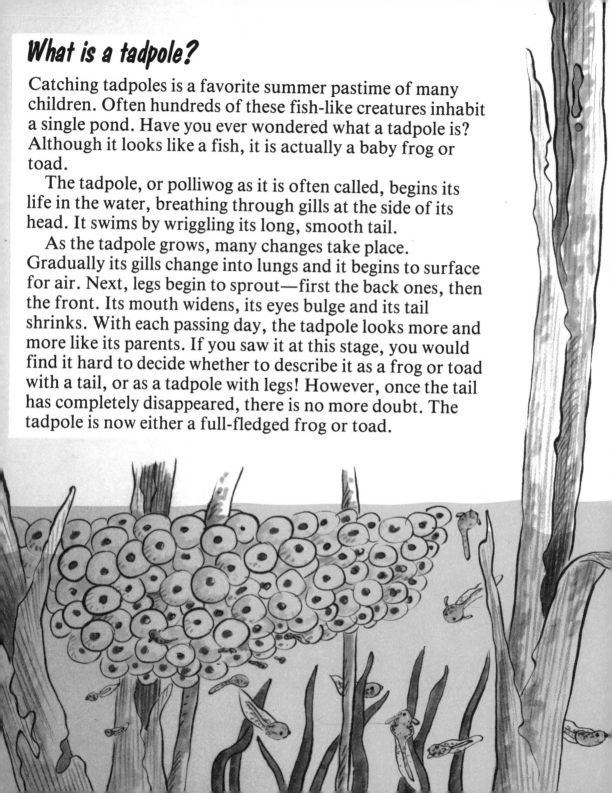

What is a tadpole?

Catching tadpoles is a favorite summer pastime of many children. Often hundreds of these fish-like creatures inhabit a single pond. Have you ever wondered what a tadpole is? Although it looks like a fish, it is actually a baby frog or toad.

The tadpole, or polliwog as it is often called, begins its life in the water, breathing through gills at the side of its head. It swims by wriggling its long, smooth tail.

As the tadpole grows, many changes take place. Gradually its gills change into lungs and it begins to surface for air. Next, legs begin to sprout—first the back ones, then the front. Its mouth widens, its eyes bulge and its tail shrinks. With each passing day, the tadpole looks more and more like its parents. If you saw it at this stage, you would find it hard to decide whether to describe it as a frog or toad with a tail, or as a tadpole with legs! However, once the tail has completely disappeared, there is no more doubt. The tadpole is now either a full-fledged frog or toad.

Do tadpoles have many enemies?

It sure isn't easy to be a tadpole. Tadpoles hatch from tiny eggs and develop slowly into frogs (or toads). Some species of frog lay thousands of eggs at a time—for a very good reason: only a few will grow into adults. All sorts of water creatures love to feast on frogs' eggs, and birds, fish, turtles and a variety of water bugs enjoy a tasty tadpole meal. And as if that weren't enough, smaller tadpoles may be eaten by bigger ones! Who needs brothers and sisters like that?

But the strangest enemy of the tadpole is actually a plant—the bladderwort. Bladderwort floats in the water and *eats* tadpoles. It

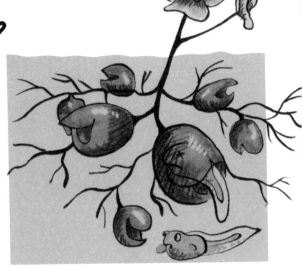

has small sacs along the edges of its leaves, and each sac has bristles and a trapdoor that opens from the bottom. The instant a tadpole rubs against the bristles, the trapdoor opens, the tadpole is sucked in and the trap snaps shut.

What iguana likes to eat flowers in the hot sun?

Most iguanas rest in the shade in the middle of the day when the sun is the hottest. But the desert iguana *(Dipsosaurus dorsalis)* sleeps in until the sun is high. Then it climbs creosote bushes so that it is above the hot ground and happily munches on fresh buds and leaves.

Can lizards fly?

The dracos or flying dragons of Southeast Asia can glide from tree to tree. These small lizards live in trees and can glide more than 8 metres (28 feet) in a downward direction. Their ''wings'' consist of skin along the sides of their body. The skin is supported by five or six long ribs between the front and the back legs. Some lizards have brightly colored ''wings'' which they use for courtship and to scare enemies as well as for gliding.

Can lizards hold their breath?

Most never even try. Some may enter the ocean occasionally but only one modern lizard lives there: the marine iguana which makes its home in the sea around the Galapagos Islands. The marine iguana eats only seaweed and may dive as deep as 15 to 20 metres (50 to 65 feet) to feed. When alarmed, it goes underwater and can stay there for up to half an hour.

What kind of lizard has three horns?

The male Jackson's chameleon has three prominent horns on its head—one by each eye and one on the snout. What for? Well, male chameleons do not like anything to get too close to them. If something does, they puff out their throat and wave their head in the air. The horns help them to look bigger and more frightening. If the intruder doesn't leave after this threat display, the chameleon charges and snaps its jaws.

29

Are snakes slimy?

Have you ever held a snake? If so, were you surprised at how it felt? Most people believe that snakes are as slimy and wet as earthworms. Nothing could be further from the truth. A snake's skin is actually very dry and feels a lot like smooth leather. However, a snake's skin shines in the sunlight, which makes it look moist. This may explain how people came to believe that snakes are slimy.

Not only is a snake's skin not wet and slimy, it is waterproof. And it repels dirt and mud as well as water, so you will never see a dirty snake.

What does cold-blooded mean?

Reptiles and amphibians are cold-blooded. This does not mean that they are always cold, but that they have no built-in control over their body temperature. The temperature of their blood changes to match that of their surroundings. Their blood is warm when the air is warm and cold when the air is cold.

Many cold-blooded animals do manage to regulate their body temperature to a certain extent by basking in the sun when they are chilled and moving into the shade or into water when they are too hot. But if their environment becomes too hot or cold, they die.

How do snakes move without feet?

A snake has more muscles than your favorite super hero! Most snakes are so strong they can hold their bodies straight out in the air with very little support. It is the snake's muscular body that enables it to move without feet.

The snake's backbone is made up of small connected bones and runs from its head to the tip of its tail. Each bone can move a little sideways and up and down. By tightening or relaxing its muscles, the snake pulls or pushes the bones, causing its whole body to move.

The underside of the snake is covered with broad, flat scales that overlap like the shingles on a roof. The scales prevent the snake from slipping backwards as it moves, like the soles of your running shoes do for you.

DID YOU KNOW . . . the fastest snake is the mamba, which can move as fast as 11 kilometres (7 miles) per hour.

Can all snakes be charmed?

Some snakes may be charming, but by no means can all snakes be charmed. Snake charmers in India usually use cobras. The snake *appears* to be charmed as it sways in time to the music of the charmer's flute. Actually, the cobra can't hear sounds carried through the air—it's just trying to keep its eyes on the snake charmer's swaying body or flute.

Are we not charming!

31

Index